Greater Than a Tourist – Wilmington, NC

50 Travel Tips from a Local

Author: Kevin Latshaw

Lock Haven, PA

ISBN: 9781521045121

DEDICATION

This book is dedicated to Lisa at CZYK Publishing for helping me put together my first published work.

BOOK DESCRIPTION

Do you want to try something new while traveling?
Do you want some guidance from locals?
Do you want to travel with the advice from a local?

If you answered yes to any of these questions then Great than a Tourist
Books are for you.

Greater Than a Tourist – Wilmington, NC by Kevin Latshaw offers the
inside scoop on Wilmington.
Most travel books tell you how to travel like a tourist. Although there's
nothing wrong with that this book will give you bucket list items to
complete, places to stay and eat on a budget or a splurge, what to do if you
are in the location for the hour or the day and much more.

In these pages you'll discover local advice that will help you throughout
your stay. Greater than a tourist is a series of travel books written by locals.
Tips from locals to tourists. Travel like a local. Get the inside scope. Slow
down, stay in one place, take your time, and get to know the people and the
culture of a place. Try some things off the beaten path with guidance.
Patronize local business and vendors when you travel. Be willing to try
something new.

By the time you finish this book, you will be excited to travel to your next
destination.
So grab YOUR copy today. You'll be glad you did.

CONTENTS

15. Enjoy dinner on the River

16. Drink a nice local brew at one of the many breweries

17. Have a great laugh at the local comedy club

18. Shop some fine stores and boutiques at Mayfaire Town Center

19. Bring your pets! A list of local hotspots that allow dogs

20. Parade around the annual Azalea Festival

21.Discover some quiet hiking trails across town

22. Enjoy the Intracoastal waterway

23. Hook some local fish at these wildlife hotspots

24. Save some money with these popular daily drink specials

25. Bring the kids to the Cape Fear Museum

26. Snake your way through the local serpenterium

27.Sleep like a local - lodging options

28.Enjoy the Carolina Beach boardwalk

29. Cheer on the UNCW seahawks at a local college atheltic match

30. Watch local theater at Thalian Hall

31. See if you are brave enough to endure a historic Ghost Tour Walk

32. Spend time not money at these free local concerts

33. Be sure to avoid these major roads during rush hour traffic

34. Best Seasonal times of the year to visit

35. Stop by these top children's attractions

Author Bio

Kevin Latshaw is a recent University of North Carolina Wilmington graduate who has lived in the area for nearly twenty years. Graduating with a degree in Communication Studies and a minor in Entrepreneurship and Innovation, Kevin has many varied interests. He loves to spend time outside with his two dogs Gus and Effy, as well as play golf and other sports.

Kevin enjoys spending his free time writing, traveling, and practicing photography. Kevin is an expert traveler who has photographed many hotspots across the United States and abroad. Internationally, Kevin has traveled and photographed such UNESCO recognized sites as Kiderdijk in The Netherlands and the Cliffs of Moher in Ireland to briefly name a few.

WELCOME TO > TOURIST

Kevin Latshaw

WHY AM I A LOCAL?

Having lived here for nearly twenty years, I can truly call myself a local.

Wilmington is a city where you can let go and relax, and enjoy all that mother nature has to offer.

In every way from the beautiful beaches, to the historic Downtown there are sights and sounds for everyone to enjoy in Wilmington.

I love Wilmington because there is always something fun to do. It could be the annual Azalea Festival Parade in April, or maybe the historic River fest in October but there is never a shortage of things to enjoy.

In Wilmington you have the luxury to play golf year round on challenging courses, or the ability to relax at one of the many area spas. No matter what, bring your friends, family, and even your pets!

While Wilmington is well known for its natural beauty, it has a laid back personality and while visiting you can enjoy some of the delicious fine dining that is around the city. Enjoy everything from fancier fare to some great inexpensive deals featuring some of Wilmington's oldest and most popular casual eateries.

Other activities to enjoy include a nice stroll around Mayfaire Town Center to browse shops and boutiques. This is where I go when I want to pick up gifts for myself or others and I never find a shortage of things to do in this area , and Wilmington as a whole.

Kevin Latshaw

1. Start Your Morning With A Great Breakfast

There are several great options when it comes to enjoying a nice breakfast in Wilmington. Whether you have a sweet tooth, or a hankering for something more savory there are places for all palates. In a rush? Grab a delicious Seahawk Bagel at local favorite establishment Beach Bagels right before the Wrightsville Beach drawbridge. In the mood for M&M waffles with whipped cream? Venture onto the island and check out the community staple Causeway Café. If you find yourself closer to midtown then definitely stop into historic Jimbo's for a traditional diner breakfast filled with staples such as eggs, bacon, hash browns, and more – located on College Road.

2. *Grab a bag of local donuts*

One thing in town that everyone can agree on is that there is only one

glazed donut that is worth the wait. They are none other than the

glazed donuts at Britt's Donuts on the Carolina Beach boardwalk. Less

than a fifteen minute drive from the heart of Wilmington, Carolina

Beach is a popular destination for its shops and popular boardwalk. If

you do have your heart set on these donuts though, be sure to bring

cash! Britt's often has a wait time between 30 minutes to an hour and

they only accept cash! Hours vary and they are only open seasonally

between the end of March through September. Don't be discouraged by

the wait, they are certainly worth it and were rated the second best in

the nation by the Small Business Association of America.

3. Eating out on a budget

While Wilmington Is home to some delicious upscale restaurants, you can eat very well without ever setting foot in them. If you don't feel like cooking there are still cheap options when going out. Check out one of the cities many locations of The Trolley Stop for their delicious hot dogs they have been serving up for years. In the mood for something else? Try stopping by Islands Tacos after 5PM where tacos are only 1$ a piece. One of my other personal favorites is the Sawmill early bird special served weekdays 3-5PM which serves up traditional home cooking favorites with two sides and a drink for less than 10$.

4. Walk The Loop like a local

Wrightsville Beach is home to "The Loop" which is a walking, jogging, and biking trail that runs along the island and lasts for nearly two and a half miles. Along the loop you will find many Wrightsville Beach and Wilmington locals walking their dogs, taking their children to the park, and surfers on their way to the waves. Feel free to bring your four legged friends and enjoy a nice refreshing walk along the breezy island of Wrightsville Beach while you take in some of its natural beauty. To enjoy this activity simply park at the Wrightsville Beach park and hop on at one of several points of the loop that surrounds the park.

5. Stroll the Historic Downtown

The Historic Downtown area of Wilmington nestled along the Cape Fear

River boasts some of the state's most popular restaurants and

attractions. There are many popular food items in this area ranging from

street fare like hot dog vendors and pizza by the slice at I Love New York

Pizza on Front Street, to fine dining such as tapas at Circa 1922 or sushi

at Yosake. There are certainly plenty of good options to be had. After a

nice meal, enjoy the famous Riverwalk which is a nice stroll down the

river where you can browse the scenery or walk into several local shops.

Pair this with numerous historic homes in the area dating back to the

1800's and there are plenty of sights to take in and enjoy in this area for

a nice afternoon or evening out.

6. Beware the parking

While the Wilmington area has many great draws such as the beaches and historic areas, there is one major setback. Parking. This has been an issue most prominently in the Wrightsville Beach and Downtown Wilmington areas , and has plagued them for years. Increasing amounts of locals and visitors have made these areas bustling during peak times, and there are not enough parking spots for everyone. Pair this with strict parking enforcement and ticketing, and it can be a nightmare. Most spaces in these locations are street metered via coins or credit/debit card and run Monday through Friday 8-6. As a cheap alternative, when downtown park in the large city of Wilmington parking deck near Market and Front Street which offers the first hour free, and then only one dollar per hour after that with a maximum price cap in place after several hours.

7. Visit one of the wonderful area parks

There is certainly no shortage of wonderful public parks in the city of

Wilmington. Popular activities include walking, jogging, skateboarding,

dog walking as well as sports such as tennis, softball, baseball, and

basketball. Popular locations include the tall pine tree filled Hugh

Macrae park wedged between Pine Grove Road and Oleander Drive.

Other options include Halyburton Park which is located on S. 17th Street.

Both of these options offer picnic tables and shelters so you can enjoy a

nice outdoor picnic. Be sure to bring your pets, as there are dog water

spouts throughout. Other popular options include Carolina Beach State

Park at Snows Cut which has a recreation area for children, as well as

areas to fish for local wildlife.

8. Venture Onto Wrightsville Beach

Previously mentioned a few times before is the municipality of

Wrightsville Beach. This small island is connected to Wilmington via a

large drawbridge that remains open, only opening for brief periods

hourly for boats to pass through. There are tons of great options for

things to do here, such as walking the loop as previously mentioned, or

stopping into Surf Berry for a healthy yogurt and fruit filled treat. If you

want something a little stronger head into local favorite Lighthouse Beer

and Wine Garden to try one of hundreds of options of local and state

beers. If you are hungry, head into the beaches own location of Mellow

Mushroom to enjoy a few slices of pizza, or even a few pretzels. If you

would like to stay on the island there are also several hotel options such

as the Blockade Runner or Holiday Inn Sunspree. For a more local vibe,

check out the listings on AirBNB and you may luck out with an

oceanfront condo or home.

9. Surf Like A Local

If you want to surf like a local then there are a few popular places to catch some waves. Try heading out to Crystal Pier at Wrightsville Beach, right next to the Oceanic restaurant. Don't get too close to the pier as that is dangerous, but pick either side next to it and shred the gnar. Depending on what time you head out you may be the only one in the line-up or just one of many local surfers – even some pro surfers reside in the Wrightsville Beach area. If you have access to a boat and want to turn things up a notch head to Masonboro Island. Just a short ride from shore the Island is home to some much bigger waves. But beware – sharks are common in this area so if that is something that worries you, steer clear!

10. Golf at some of the areas nicest courses

Wilmington is home to numerous fine golf courses. From high dollar award winning courses, to cheaper neighborhood friendly courses there are options for all skill levels and groups. Bring the family out to Echo Farms Golf Club to enjoy a modestly priced round on a very nice and challenging course. Conditions are well kept up throughout the year, and other than maybe a brief winter freeze in December or January you should be able to play year round. If you are more of a serious golfer, try to arrange a tee time at Beau Rivage. Prices are a little higher, but this upscale course has all the bells and whistles. Everything from GPS range finders in the carts, to beverage service on the course is available. Be sure to inquire about student, senior, or other possible discounts if applicable.

Kevin Latshaw

"The ocean stirs the heart, inspires the imagination and brings eternal joy to the soul" – Robert Wyland

11. Enjoy Mother Nature at Airlie Gardens

If you have a hankering to see some more natural beauty including an oak tree that is over five hundred years old then be sure to head to Airlie Gardens. The park was originally commissioned over one hundred years ago as a private garden, but has since been transformed into the areas most intricately maintained public garden. Open for general admission Tuesday through Sunday enjoy the many various exhibits the gardens boasts such as stained glass pieces as well as statues and even annual light shows such as Enchanted Airlie in December.

12. Have a drink, or a few at the Beach Bars

While the Wilmington area may have many attractions that bring

visitors to the area, one of the most popular draws is certainly a string

of local bars creatively named by the locals "The Beach Bars". Nestled

onto Wrightsville Beach and popular on Thursday, Friday, and Saturday

evenings these bars can include Red Dogs, Banks Channel, Jimmy's,

Lagerheads, 22 North, and Neptune's. All feature their own unique

characteristics, for example Jimmy's often has live music. All of them

feature good drink specials, but they can get extremely crowded during

the summer season so beware. Most locals finish up at the bars by 2AM

and then head to Vito's which is right next door to some of the bars and

they grab a slice or even a whole pie to take home. The pizza is excellent

and a great way to end a fun night.

13. Tour the USS North Carolina Battleship

One of the areas most interesting and family friendly historical

attractions is anchored downtown in the Cape Fear River. The USS

Battleship North Carolina was a World War Two era battleship that was

decommissioned and permanently harbored here in 1961. Weighing in

at about 36,000 tons this massive floating ship features tours, birthday

parties, even holiday themed events. If you dare, be sure to visit in

October for "The Haunted Battleship" experience which is a ghost tour

led around the ship at night while discussing some of the ghoulish

sailors that still roam the ship to this day.

14. Step back in time at the Cotton Exchange Shopping Center

Located in the heart of the Downtown Wilmington Historic district is the popular Cotton Exchange Shopping Center. This dining and shopping destination has several entrances that encompass the multiple structure historical complex. Originally a flour mill in the early 1900's this piece of Wilmington history now houses specialty shops such as Cape Fear Beads & Gemstones which offers handmade jewelry pieces. Brick walkways connect the various shops and buildings and once you finish shopping be sure to hang around for lunch. One of the most popular spots would be the German Café which has been there for years serving up delicious Rueben sandwiches and desserts such as German Chocolate cake.

15. Enjoy Dinner on the River

The Cape Fear Riverwalk features some excellent waterfront options for dining. For fancier fare or a romantic date be sure to stop into Riverboat Landing. This establishment has been around for over thirty years and has a famous set of individual upstairs balconies, with tables overlooking the river. Be sure to make a reservation though, as these can be very popular. If you can't take advantage of those great seats, head to popular restaurant The George for another great view paired with upscale dining, appetizers, and drinks. The restaurant is located on the famous Riverwalk and offers excellent seafood. While most patrons drive their cars and park in the outside parking lot, if you would prefer you can drive your boat and dock it while enjoying your meal.

16. Have a local brew from one of the many breweries

Wilmington will never run out of beer with all the fantastic local

breweries that are in the area. Being a hip and trendy community the

craft beer scene has erupted and a surge of small independent

breweries followed. Check out local favorite Front Street Brewery and

even take a tour before having a nice lunch or dinner. Other good

downtown options include Flytrap Brewery which makes its own brews.,

as well as Ironclad Brewery. If you still want more options there are

many more delicious breweries to try. On Kerr Avenue there is

Wilmington Brewing Company, and another popular favorite in town is

Waterline Brewing Company. Each location will have its own personality

and atmosphere as well as a plethora of local homemade beers and

microbrews to test out.

17. Have a laugh at the local comedy club

Dead Crow Comedy Room located in Downtown Wilmington features some of the funniest acts that the town has ever had. Located on Front Street this joint is only open in the evenings and features nightly programs and rotating comedians on the weekend. While they receive big names that come through town, most notably though is their open mic night on Thursday which is always a fun time. Paired with drink specials and finger foods like pizza rolls and bagel bites this is a fun place to be. Beware, arrive early as they often fill to capacity and if that happens you will have to wait until people leave before you can be let in.

18. Shop stores and boutiques in Mayfaire Town Center

If you like to shop, or maybe get a massage, or see an iMax movie then Mayfaire Town Center should be on list of places to visit. Comprised of hundreds of shops, restaurants and retailers there is plenty to do. Enjoy a coffee and a magazine inside Barnes and Noble, or walk over to Regal Cinemas and catch a new movie. Once you finish up, try having lunch at Tokyo 101 for Japanese cuisine and sushi. If that's not your style, hit up Fox and Hound for traditional bar food as well as daily food and drink specials. It also features a grocery store, a Fresh Market, a fitness gym, and many other useful amenities.

19. Pets Welcome! Local Hotspots that accept dogs

Most restaurants allow dogs when sitting outside on the patio, and many even offer dog bowls for water. If you and your pooch want more then water, be sure to visit the Goat and Compass bar downtown which frequently has four legged friends visiting inside. Also a popular location in the downtown area is Satellite bar and lounge which also allows animals to accompany their owners. In addition, there are even places that were made for dogs. Check out some of the local dog parks to let you pup blow off steam. There are dog parks at both Hugh Macrae and Empie Park, which are divided one section for smaller dogs and one section for larger dogs. If you and your dog want to hit the beach feel free, but not during the months of April-September. These months are prohibited for pets on the actual sand portion of Wrightsville Beach.

20. Visit During the Annual Azalea Festival

The first or second week of April Wilmington usually hosts the North

Carolina Azalea festival. This festival offers a parade, a street fair, free

concerts, and then ticketed headlining concerts in the evenings that are

reasonably priced. The best tip about the festival is that the parade is

absolutely a huge affair, when you combine this with the slim parking

downtown it can create a nightmare. If possible, get dropped off and

leave your vehicle parked somewhere else, try uber or a cab if

necessary. If you do end up having to drive there will be scalpers selling

parking spots at private businesses. This is normal, and completely safe

and legal and they were given permission and could be your only bet at

getting a space within miles walking distance of the parade. I suggest

paying the fee of 20-30$ that they may be charging, or just getting a ride

ahead of time to save some cash. Be sure to arrive early to grab one of

these spots and bring a lawn chair to enjoy the parade. Then afterwards

hit the street fair and check out local arts and crafts as well as food

vendors.

Kevin Latshaw

"Broad, wholesome, charitable views of men and things cannot be acquired by vegetating in one little corner of the earth all one's lifetime"
- Mark Twain

Kevin Latshaw

21. Discover some quiet hiking trails

While not an urban metropolis, Wilmington can be busy during certain times of the year or if there is a large event in town. If you want to escape the crowds and enjoy some time to yourself try going on a short hike on one of the nature trails scattered around town. Usually found in parks or nature reserves these easy hikes are simply walks around the great outdoors that are quite relaxing and quiet. Halyburton park has various trails for you to try, and if you prefer walking on the sidewalk you could always follow one of those walking routes along the park. If you prefer more of a secluded nature hike there is an option located at the Carolina Beach State Park titled the Sugarloaf trail. This roughly three mile trail winds through the trees and forest and has some nice sights and sounds. Following along the riverbed you get to experience some of the nearby marsh as well for a good feeling of the tidal community.

22. Enjoy the Intracoastal Waterway

Two popular activities that locals frequently enjoy other than surfing,

include kayaking and paddle boarding in the Intracoastal Waterway. The

Intracoastal Waterway is an inland body of water that runs in between

the land and the Atlantic ocean. This combination of rivers, and inlets is

more stable than being offshore in the stronger currents. This calmer

body of water is great for kayaking and paddle boarding without having

to battle the waves as much. Kayaking is the traditional method where

you are seated and paddling in your small boat, but paddle boarding is

where you stand straight up and row while atop a large flat board

similar to a surfboard. Other popular activities you can enjoy include

raft tubing behind a boat, or renting jet ski's. Be sure to be careful in the

busier summer month as the waterway can become crowded so be sure

to leave safe distances between other boaters if going tubing or

enjoying other activities.

23. Hook some local fish at these hotspots

The good news for seafood lovers is that you can catch a multitude of fish pretty much anywhere in Wilmington. Whether it be ponds, rivers, the ocean, or just off a dock there are plenty of ways to catch and eat some delicious fish that you bring in. Many locals enjoy surf fishing at less populated portions of Carolina Beach, or even Masonboro Island by simply casting a reel out into the surf and seeing what comes back. Other popular options include fishing off of the Carolina Beach Pier which allows fishermen and women to go deeper into the water. If you have access to a boat simply cast a line anywhere in the Intracoastal or Cape Fear River and try to look for the shade around land structures where fish like to hide. Other popular options include offshore charter fishing where it is a much more serious affair. Be sure to stock up on bait and tackle at popular local destination Intracoastal Angler on Oleander Drive. Featuring live bait along with numerous rods, reels, and supplies they will get you up and running.

24. Save some money with these daily drink specials

Drinking is a longtime favorite pastime in Wilmington and you can usually find a good drink special regardless of what night it is. This is in part due to the large college crowd from UNCW but many businesses around campus, the Downtown area, and the beaches participate. If you find yourself in the Wrightsville Beach area on a Monday check out Bank's Channel for 1$ PBR's and Lagerheads for 2$ domestic bottles. On Tuesday nights head to Might as Well on Racine Drive for 1$ select draft beers. On Wednesday's restaurant Kickback Jack's has all of their domestic pints on sale for $2.75. For more of a club scene on Thursday night you can head upstairs while at the Liquidroom to dance, or you can just sit at the bar downstairs and enjoy $3 Red Bull vodka's. If you like Fireball whiskey, stop by Carolina Ale House next to UNCW on College Road for $4 Fireballs any day of the week. These are only some of the local drink specials, and most locals have their own favorite special in town that they frequent.

25. Bring the kids to the Cape Fear Museum

The Cape Fear Children's museum is a wonderful resource that

Wilmington offers for families and their little ones. Located in

Downtown Wilmington on Orange Street the large museum caters

specifically to a younger age range from about 6-15 years old. Featuring

rotating monthly and seasonal exhibits and activities the offerings

change but there are some permanent fixtures that are always

enjoyable. Some of the rotating activities include a children's cooking

club, as well as things such as DINO Day. Other fun play fixtures inside

include a pirate ship and a grocery store for children to have fun with.

26. Snake your way through the Serpentarium

Located on Orange Street in Downtown Wilmington is the Cape Fear

Serpentarium which is home to over eighty species of rare and

dangerous reptiles. Some of the more popular exhibits include the

anacondas, pythons, and boa constrictors. In addition, this location is

home to multiple giant crocodiles. Be sure to take the kids for a fun

afternoon walk through the Serpentarium and then finish the evening

with a nice dinner in the nearby historic district. Nearly next door to the

Serpentarium is the delicious fondue restaurant The Little Dipper. Enjoy

multiple courses of delicious food, fruit, and vegetables at one of

Wilmington's most popular restaurants without the hassle of a long

walk.

27. Sleep in comfort - Best local lodging options

Some of the best lodging options in the area will cost a pretty penny.

These include top dollar hotels such as the Hilton Riverside, or the

Holiday Inn Sunspree. If its in the budget I would highly recommend

either of these hotels for their excellent locations and service. But, if

you want to stay more like a local then be sure to employ the use of

lodging site AirBNB. This site allows you to stay in local residents homes

at a fraction of the price of hotels. Not only will this tactic save you

money and provide you with excellent lodging accommodations, but it

also can provide the potential of meeting great local hosts as well.

28. Take a walk down the Carolina Beach boardwalk

The Carolina Beach boardwalk is a popular destination for tourists and their families. Home to local gems such as Britt's donuts, as mentioned in a previous chapter, the boardwalk boasts many fun shops and good eateries. In addition, there is the amusement park section of the boardwalk which has small rides for children. Be sure to go at night to enjoy the free firework display each Thursday at sundown during the summer months.

29. Try to catch a UNCW Seahawk Athletic match

UNCW is home to many talented athletic teams both men and women's

and they play sports ranging from basketball, baseball, softball, to

soccer and track and field. Catch a basketball game at Trask Coliseum

during the college basketball season , or even participate in the annual

Midnight Madness event that kicks off each season. UNCW Men's

basketball team won the CAA conference in 2016 and 2017, thus

participating in the NCAA men's Basketball tournament each year. If you

prefer to stay outside try to watch a men's or women's soccer game.

The teams are highly ranked each year and contain many young stars

that are exciting to watch. Paired with a positive college atmosphere

these games are always inexpensive to purchase tickets and fun to

attend.

30. Watch local theater at Historic Thalian Hall

Originally constructed in 1855 this large building was once used as city

hall and has since undergone a five million dollar renovation to handle

more annual visitors. They offer live theater and shows that are

excellently rated. In addition to small local theater productions Thalian

Hall also acts as an arts hub that screens historical movies as well as

current top rated documentaries. Located in Downtown Wilmington on

Chestnut Street be sure to park curbside if there isn't room in their

parking lot, and remember to check their website for their current

offerings.

"The world is a book, and those who do not travel read only one page."
– Saint Augustine

31. See if you are brave enough for a Ghost Tour

Officially titled as the Ghost Walk of Old Wilmington, this popular tour boasts many stories that even some locals haven't heard unless they have personally taken this tour themselves. Usually running nightly around 6:30 (except in the winter months of January and February) this tour meets at the corner of Market and Water Streets. While young children under six years old are free, the cost for adults is around ten dollars but it is certainly worth it. This hour and a half journey tours Historic Wilmington's most haunted areas and visits some of the darker stories of the towns past. The guides are incredibly intelligent, and excellent storytellers. If you can't quite handle the goose bumps then alternatively look into a daytime history walking tour also starting downtown on the riverfront similar to the ghost tour.

32. Spend Time Not Money at these Free concerts

One of the best parts of Wilmington are some of the free activities that

you can enjoy. If you visit in the summer months between May and

September there are free weekly concerts downtown on Friday

evenings. Known to locals as the downtown sundown concerts these

feature free bands so you can save your money for other things. Be sure

to check out my personal favorite of the series, the Dave Matthews

Tribute Band.

33. Avoid these major roads during rush hour traffic

One thing that can ruin a vacation is sitting in awful traffic for hours.

While Wilmington is nothing compared to other major cities in the U.S.,

the roads can still get quite congested at peak times. Known to locals is

College Road which is a long road that runs through a majority of

midtown Wilmington. Avoid this road at all costs between the hours of

5PM and 6PM, the traffic can be quite terrible. Another set of traffic

concerns to be aware of are the bridge openings for Wrightsville Beach.

The Bridge usually opens hourly, on the hour to let boats pass through.

This really backs up traffic going to and from the island. Occasionally

there will be additional openings that you can't plan for but these can

create quite a traffic backup on Eastwood Road heading towards

Wrightsville Beach, or vice versa.

34. Best Time of the year to visit

While there are no bad times to visit Wilmington, some may argue that April or May are the nicest months out of the year weather wise. With temperatures usually in the mid 70's to mid 80's these months are warm, but not as humid and stiflingly hot as the late summer months of July and August. If you visit in the first week of April you can partake in the local tradition of the Azalea Festival and all that it entails. If you do come at a different time don't worry there are fun events year round. The iconic and mega popular local Lighthouse Beer & Wine Festival takes place in October and offers ticketholders the chance to sample over 70 different types of beers. If you visit during the holiday season in December try to pick up tickets for local favorite Enchanted Airlie which turns beautiful Airlie Gardens into a decorated and well-lit winter Wonderland.

35. *Do not miss these top children's attractions*

There are many fun stops for the kids in Wilmington, whether it be the local Jungle Rapids entertainment park, or the brand new super awesome Battle House Laser Tag area. If the kids want go karts, a water park, a huge arcade, a café, mini golf, as well as climbing walls then be sure to stop by Jungle Rapids on Oleander. Around for years this place has many fun activities that everyone will enjoy. If you want to go somewhere specifically to blow off some steam hit up state of the art Battle House Laser Tag on Hall Drive. Other fun children's attractions include the Cape Fear Children's museum which should be taken into consideration, as well as Mayfaire Town Center which has an iMax movie theater.

36. Utilize these safe and fun transportation methods

Wilmington has plenty of convenient, unique, and fun transportation methods for getting around. Want to cruise on the river? Then try Cape Fear River Cruises. Want to trot around the downtown area? Then hire one of the multiple horse drawn carriages that are available for rides. Also available in the downtown area is a free hop on and off trolley whose route can be found online. In the mood for something a little more modern? Try an Uber for a low rate when taxi's are unavailable, but beware – local surge rates can get pretty expensive as well at peak times. Want to be eco friendly? Look for one of the several golf cart taxi's around the beach bars if you are staying close by. Or in true local fashion, grab a long board skateboard and go for a ride.

37. Handling ILM International Airport

Wilmington International Airport is small and only has a few gates, however at certain times of the year can get quite busy. There are a few expert tips to navigating the airport quickly and efficiently. When you land at ILM be sure to call an Uber as the plane touches down to cut down on the 15 drive for them to get to the airport. When departing from Wilmington try to take advantage of mobile boarding passes to avoid waiting in lengthy lines at the ticket counters. Try to bring your own food, things are quite overpriced when you cross the security clearance area even water. Bring a refillable water bottle to take advantage of water fountains and free water. If trying to redeem miles look into Delta and American Airlines as they are the two carriers that service ILM. If flying privately and not commercially be sure to contact local company Seahawk Aviation to take care of your every needs for jets and charter service.

38. Planning for the Wilmington Weather

The weather in Wilmington can be very unpredictable. The morning may start out clear and sunny, but by the afternoon rain showers may have rolled in; especially during the summer months. For that reason alone, always have a rain coat handy and a back up activity planned as well. For the most part however, Wilmington's weather can be humid, sunny, and moderately warm most of the spring and summer. There is always a lot of moisture in the air so be prepared to deal with hair malfunctions at times. In the winter things can actually get pretty chilly and right around the freezing mark. Be sure to pack some warm clothing if visiting between November and February. It's also a good idea to usually carry around a light jacket, as sometimes when the weather does fluctuate businesses and restaurants struggle to regulate their inside temperatures and they bounce between too hot or too cold. If allergies bother you, be sure to take an allergy pill if visiting in March, or April. The pollen in the area can be extremely bad at these times.

39. Visit these Downtown Bars

Other than restaurants, bars are certainly the most numerous business located in the downtown area. Local patrons have the luxury of visiting multiple bars each time they go out, thus getting to experience many different sides of the Downtown Wilmington area. For a relaxed drink be sure to stop by Blue Post and play a game of pool or darts. If you prefer an authentic Irish pub then stop by Slainte, located on Front street. If you want some live music, stop by the Whiskey on the corner of Front and Market. If you are in more of a mood for a club atmosphere then stop by The Liquid Room which is a two story bar and nightclub that will certainly entertain on a Friday or Saturday evening. If you want to dance in one of the fancier clubs downtown then stop by Pravda which boasts DJ's as well as bottle service. If you are really feeling the North Carolina Spirit then stop by City Limits Saloon for a drink with a country twist, and even ride the mechanical bull if you're feeling up for it!

40. Eating the best burger in town doesn't break the bank

When it comes to the best burger in town be sure to visit P.T's Olde

Fashioned Grille. This area favorite has been around for many years and

has now evolved into numerous locations throughout the area. Choose

from the 4oz or the 8oz famous burger and of course it is paired with

the fries, which may be even more famous than the burger. Add in a

drink and you're looking at a total of about 8$, and for that price you

can't beat the delicious taste. If you prefer something lighter take

advantage of their equally delicious turkey sandwich that is warmed up

on the griddle. My recommendation, be sure to add bacon on top

regardless of what you're ordering. Stop by the location on Oleander

Drive before or after a trip to the beach.

Kevin Latshaw

"You don't have to be rich to travel well." – *Eugene Fodor*

41. Stock up at the best grocery stores in the area

There is certainly no shortage of grocery stores in the area. There are popular chain grocery stores such as Harris Teeter, Publix, and Trader Joes. There are also the common staple big box stores such as Walmart, Sam's Club and Target. For a more localized shop, try the Tidal Market on Oleander Drive which is a healthy grocery store serving up organics and other fresh specialty items. If you are looking for specialty Italian grocery store items try a Taste of Italy on college road for authentic Italian food as well as a large selection of grocery items.

42. Check out some of the sweet rides at Cars and Coffee

Local car enthusiasts know where the largest meet is each week. Cars

and Coffee is a nation wide trend where locals get together on Saturday

mornings for a few hours to show off their sport and aftermarket cars. If

you want to stop by and check out some of the coolest local cars in the

area then head to the Chili's parking lot on College Road. But, wake up

early or else you'll miss it. A lot of the cars start to leave around 11AM.

Some of the cars that stop by include BMW, Volkswagen and Porsche

sport cars as well as muscle cars such as the Ford Mustang. Of course

most of these rides will feature aftermarket parts and modified engines

and exteriors that will be sure to impress. Don't be intimidated though,

most owners are very friendly and will let you poke around and check

them out thoroughly.

43. Fill up your gas tanks at these frequently cheap stations

When on road trips travelers tend to purchase a lot of gas. These fuel purchases add up, and being able to fill up for the lowest price available can make a difference when purchasing large quantities. In Wilmington the cheapest gas is usually found on College Road at Sam's Club. You do need a Sam's membership, so if you don't have one then this won't be the option for you; however don't fret there are still other good options. Also on College Road is the Go Gas Station which is open to anyone, and its bright red pumps usually have some of the lowest prices in town. If you require premium gasoline and prefer Shell stations there are plenty of them offering their popular V-Power fuel around town, including on Eastwood Road as well as Carolina Beach Road.

44. *Spend an afternoon at the ballpark*

The Wilmington Sharks, a talented summer baseball league team have been in town for twenty years and their games are always a fun way to spend an afternoon or evening. The games have a nice relaxed ballpark atmosphere that is ideal for a baseball fan or a family. With drink specials, as well as food options this is certainly not just a small time game. Opening day for the team is usually at the end of May, so be sure to check them out at Legion Stadium on Carolina Beach Road. Home to the sharks, the field portion of the sports complex is often referred to by locals as "The Shark Tank".

45. Check out the Fort Fisher aquarium

The Fort Fisher Aquarium is a wonderful option for taking the children

for a fun activity, or simply spending a nice relaxing day or afternoon.

Usually open from nine to five each day, this popular attraction is not

only a fun destination but also a service that helps marine and aquatic

life in the area through their volunteer and research work. Located at

the far end of Carolina Beach, technically in what is called Kure Beach

there lies Fort Fisher and the aquarium. The aquarium boasts exhibits

featuring sharks, stingrays, fish, eels as well as many more species and

interactive games and activities.

46. Grub out late with these late night eateries

If there is one thing Wilmington knows how to do, it is eat. Even very late at night you can satisfy your cravings without lifting a pot or a pan. Check out popular Slice of Life Pizza located in Downtown Wilmington on Market Street. Open until 3AM this pizza will certainly fill you up and satisfy some of those late night desires. Local diner Jimbo's opens at 10PM each night and closes at 2PM in the afternoon. This spot has been around for years and has a large local fanbase. Depending on when you stop in, you're very likely to see Jimbo himself, the owner sitting at the counter. If you want food but don't want to drive there are even late night delivery services. Have a hankering for a dozen warm chocolate chip cookies to be delivered to your door? Call up Insomnia Cookies near the University. Their delivery hours run from about midday to 3AM. Finally, if you still haven't satisfied those cravings be sure to call up Munchies in University Landing next to UNCW. Get one of their classic sandwiches delivered and pair it with their fried Oreos for dessert.

47. Enjoy a concert at Greenfield Lake Amphitheater

If your idea of a relaxing afternoon is listening to some good music in a relaxed atmosphere while possibly enjoying a beer or two, then Greenfield Lake Amphitheater is the place for you. This small venue near the Downtown Wilmington area hosts various musical acts ranging from The Tedeschi Trucks band to bigger names such as Willie Nelson. This open air venue is surrounded by trees and near a small local lake and makes for a peaceful concert atmosphere with both seats and standing room. The sound quality remains excellent despite its outside setup, and the alcohol prices are not as marked up and as expensive as many larger venues that travelers may have been to before.

48. Browse some trendy fine art in these galleries

Wilmington has an up and coming art scene that has recently been

bolstered by the opening of some new downtown galleries. Historically,

the Cameron Art Museum was the first opened in town back in 1964

and is located off 17th Street near Shipyard Boulevard. Featuring several

rotating exhibits, as well as a clay studio and several art and education

classes this location also has a nice café for visitors. However more

recently newer galleries have opened such as Acme Art located

downtown, which is a collection of various artists that host an open to

the public exhibition every fourth Friday of the month. While not an art

gallery, another fun local option to walk through includes the Blue

Moon Gift shop on Racine Drive. Rated the best area gift shop for the 9th

year in a row by local Encore magazine, this shop stocks local art,

pottery, hand-blown glass, and jewelry.

49. Strike up a good time at these fun bowling alleys

If bad weather such as rain hampers your outside activities for the day it is always smart to have a backup plan. Bowling is a great game to play for fun with your children, or even with friends as a more serious competition. This game is easy for anyone to learn and Wilmington features a newly renovated Bowling Alley that is sure to impress beginners and experts alike. Ten Pin Alley off College Road has recently been updated with new electronics and lanes. Also including billiards and food and drinks as well this location is a must visit if you plan to do some bowling. If you find yourself at the opposite end of town however try out the old faithful Cardinal Lanes on Shipyard. Around for years this 32 lane bowling alley has hosted many veteran bowlers throughout the years.

50. Catch a Hammerheads Soccer Game

The Wilmington Hammerheads are a semi-professional soccer team that have been in the area for over twenty years. Also located in Legion stadium, the team has regularly played against MLS teams in various competitions throughout the years. Guaranteed for a fun afternoon or evening, the atmosphere is excellent and the crowd does a great job of supporting the local team. Be sure to grab a popcorn while enjoying the outdoor weather and cheer on the home team during the fast paced action. Be on the look out for free shirts being handed out to the crowd as well.

> Tourist

Greater than a Tourist

Please read other Greater than a Tourist Books

Join the >Tourist Mailing List :
http://eepurl.com/cxspyf

Facebook:
https://www.facebook.com/GreaterThanATourist/

Please leave your honest review of this book on Amazon and Goodreads. Thank you.

Made in the USA
Columbia, SC
18 January 2021